God
Really, Really
Likes You

Everyday Lessons in Faith

BECKY PROCTOR

WESTBOW
PRESS®
A DIVISION OF THOMAS NELSON
& ZONDERVAN

WestBow Press books may be ordered through booksellers or by contacting:

WestBow Press
A Division of Thomas Nelson & Zondervan
1663 Liberty Drive
Bloomington, IN 47403
www.westbowpress.com
844-714-3454

ISBN: 978-1-6642-5106-9 (sc)
ISBN: 978-1-6642-5105-2 (hc)
ISBN: 978-1-6642-5107-6 (e)

Library of Congress Control Number: 2021924079

Print information available on the last page.

WestBow Press rev. date: 12/30/2021

To anyone who has ever felt unloved, unwanted, or not good enough, I dedicate this book in the name of the Father, the Son, and the Holy Spirit.

Contents

When Someone Likes You

LET ME ASK you a question: how do you feel when you hear that someone likes you? Do you smile at the thought? I'm not surprised. Being liked by another person gets your attention, doesn't it? It's flattering. Regardless of your age, knowing someone likes you feels nice. Oxytocin and other chemicals flood your brain, giving you those warm and fuzzy sensations. Then, after the initial reaction, you likely will become curious. In my experience, another person's interest in me results in my becoming interested in them. Who is this person? I want to know more. In some instances, mutual admiration develops into friendship. Some may last for a season; others, for a lifetime.

What about when the "person" who likes you is God?

Can we really compare making a new friend with making God that new friend? Sort of but not really. I say this because people, our earthly friends, cannot measure up to the friendship that God offers. People are fallible. Regardless of our best intentions, circumstances of life intervene. For example, I promised myself I would be at my friend Beverly's bedside when she took her last breath. She battled ovarian cancer for nearly seven years, but restrictions imposed by COVID prevented my being with her in her final hours here on earth. But God was with her. Throughout her illness, Bev's hope was in God and His constant presence.

You may be surprised to learn that God and I haven't always

been on speaking terms. It took me years to accept the idea that God really, really likes me. I was a child who didn't ask many questions. From bits and pieces of fundamentalist sermons and overheard conversations, my image of God was anything but loving. I pictured God as the enforcer, the disapprover, a bad Santa, ready to catch me doing something "bad." If life were a game of Whack-a-Mole, I was the mole and God the mallet wielder. I feared God, so no way was I going to trust Him. Not surprisingly, I did not want to get to know God. He would only judge and condemn me, and I managed to do that quite well on my own. As I was nearing middle age, my attitude began to soften. Coincidentally, about this same time, I began to realize that many of the "normal" people around me were people of faith. Were they new to faith, I wondered, or was I just beginning to notice? This kinder, gentler me decided that if someone could provide me with the formula, read the verses, pray the prayer, and allow me to ride into heaven on the coattails of their personal faith, I was in. I was soon to learn the truth about faith: you must do it alone.

The motivation to get connected to God must come from deep within, from your spiritual self. We all have one, you know; we are not simply flesh and blood. The desire to know God may feel like a hunger that cannot be satisfied or a yearning that defies description. I've heard it said that each of us has a hole in us in the shape of God. We try to fill it with relationships, food, drugs or alcohol, expensive toys, entertainment, and more, but the hole is still there. When we let go of our egos and realize we are not in control of our lives, we can surrender and allow God to fill that space within.

From whence did my motivation come? It came within the first year of my marriage to an adorable man who God handpicked to be my husband. Our meeting, courtship, and marriage were definitely a "God thing"—that is a story for another day—but I was totally unprepared for marriage, my first, at age forty. Over and over, I kept thinking, *I don't know how to do this!* People often hit rock bottom in one form or another before they remember to look heavenward, and that's how it happened with me. My frustration reached a crescendo one night, and I fell to my knees on the bedroom carpet, praying, "God, You've sent me this wonderful husband, but I am going to make a mess of this marriage if You don't help me. Please, please, take over my life. I can't do it anymore." Not the most eloquent of prayers but an honest, straight-from-the-heart humble confession and supplication.

That night, God and I connected for real. Nothing in my life up to that point had been wasted because God is always working behind the scenes. God may have begun this book in me when I was ten years old. Always a reader, I began to write stories then—stories that, throughout the years, have been misplaced and lost. And I never stopped writing, from newspaper reporter to technical writer to blogger. Now, it thrills me to share some of the lessons I have learned along the way.

It has been an emotional experience. One morning, I sat at my laptop. My fingers hovered over the keys. I felt a burning in my nose as tears filled my eyes. In my heart, I began to pray, *Only one. Only one. Lord, give me the words to help just one person understand how much You care. How much You not only love them, but like them. Only one.*

The stories that follow are true accounts of lessons God has taught me through daily living, Bible verses, and other "languages" I understand. He speaks to me through people of all ages, lifestyles, and social and economic status. Sometimes they even use words! You may hear His voice through music or poetry, through sermons and studies, through the wind and rain and sea and sky. Even in silence, you will hear Him. Especially in silence.

When someone calls what I do a *ministry*, I am humbled. I confess there are only a few of the Ten Commandments that I have not broken and will probably continue to break during my lifetime, but our loving and merciful God forgives and restores me. Although He does not take pleasure in my sin, He uses every misstep, every minute aspect of my sin, to equip me to serve Him better. I take no credit for anything I do. God has ordered my steps, given me gifts and talents, moved people in and out of my life, and provided opportunities I could not have orchestrated on my own. It is my prayer that God will continue to use me to His glory for as long as I live.

I invite you to walk with me awhile. This is not your typical inspirational book. I am neither biblical scholar nor teacher. I am a writer but not one who labors for hours over sentence structure and punctuation. It's just me, moving through my days, trying to pay attention, looking, listening, and waiting for God to appear in the ordinary, everyday circumstances of life. As you turn the pages, you may smile or chuckle, but I pray you'll never forget that God is always available to you and, regardless of what anyone says, God really, really likes you.

God Really Does Like You

God created humans in His image. In the image of
God He created them.

—Genesis 1:27 (God's Word Translation)

GOD REALLY, REALLY likes you.

Did you know that?

Let me say it again.

God really, *really* likes *you*.

I'll bet my booties you've never heard those words. Oh yes,
you've heard "God loves you," so frequently, perhaps, that it goes
in one ear and out the other. Just another cliché, like "Have a nice
day!" and "How are you?"

The word *love* is so overused these days. After all, I love my
husband and my family; I love my friends; I love razzleberry pie;
I love a good book; I love my pets; I love line-dried bed sheets;
and I love watching the sun rise. Does God love me as much or
more than I love Häagen-Dazs ice cream?

My family of origin isn't shy about saying, "I love you." One
day, however, my mom looked at me out of the blue and said, in
the sweetest little mom voice, "I like you." Time seemed to stand

still, as often it does when something life-altering happens. My heart turned a somersault as those feel-good hormones flooded my brain. "I like you too!" I chirped back, grinning from ear to ear. Yes, I knew my mother loved me, but to hear that she *liked* me validated me on so many levels. So does knowing that God likes me.

Why is it that so many of us feel that He doesn't?

Several years ago, my good friend Mary Lee confessed she felt that way. Mary Lee and I had met years earlier. She was on the newspaper's society desk, and I was a reporter. I was twenty-four, and she was in her late forties, with three teenagers at home and a husband who traveled for work. Despite the age difference, we became the best of friends. According to her husband, Bob, they maintained their youthful outlook by always having young friends. It worked.

This particular morning, Mary Lee and I were sitting in her car outside Ukrop's in Richmond, Virginia, drinking French roast coffee and gobbling down warm glazed doughnuts, when God entered into the conversation.

She took a sip of her coffee, cast her eyes downward, and solemnly said, "You know, Becky, I don't think God likes me very much." She looked so sad.

Heartsick, I felt her pain keenly. I reached for her hand and held it in mine as I responded. "Oh, Mary, God doesn't just like you. He absolutely adores you! You are His favorite. Don't you know that? You, my friend, are His custom design, created in His image. No one else is like you. You are that special."

That's the message I want to leave you with today, dear reader. No matter how raggedy, how despicable you are feeling, God likes you *and* loves you. He created you in His own image. You are not some randomly occurring experiment or some fatally flawed lump of humanity. You are not a victim of your circumstances, or of another's bad decisions, or someone else's selfish dreams. You are God's own creation.

The Bible, in all of its many translations, is timeless and alive with wisdom and spiritual truth. Eugene Peterson's book *Eat This Book* invites us to dine on the Word. The first bite I recommend is Genesis 1:27.

Let's do this. Read the following aloud: "I was created in God's image." Read it a few more times, emphasizing a different word each time. Copy it down on paper. Hang it on your bathroom mirror, and read it out loud daily.

Words, spoken aloud, are powerful.

You, my friend, are God's custom design, created for a purpose much greater than you could ever imagine. The journey of faith is one of adventure, joy, creativity, and hope. Your heart will expand with tenderness and compassion, and your spirit will soar to heavenly heights. You will be stronger than you ever imagined, and you will, indeed, perform miracles beyond anything you could ever do on your own (see John 1:12).

Good and gracious God, empower us to demonstrate Your love to all humankind. Let us be Your hands and feet to walk in Your will to the glory of Your name. Amen.

A Heavenly Scent

But thanks be to God, Who always leads us in triumphal procession in Christ, and through us spreads everywhere the fragrance of the knowledge of Him.

—2 Corinthians 2:14 (Amplified Bible)

HAVE YOU EVER walked through a neighborhood and caught a whiff of fresh laundry? There's just something about that fragrance wafting out from an unseen dryer vent that lifts my heart and puts a smile on my face. It's one of life's little pleasures, reminding me of crisp white sheets, a cozy blanket still warm from the dryer, or a loving hug from someone wearing a freshly laundered shirt.

Repeatedly, the Old Testament speaks of God being pleased by the "aroma" of the offerings made on behalf of His people for the atonement of sin. Mostly, I think about burnt offerings. How surprised I was to find that certain verses in the New Testament describe followers of Jesus not only as a pleasing "aroma," but as "a sweet perfume that brings Christ to everyone" (2 Corinthians 2:15 Contemporary English Version).

Imagine it. As we travel through life, we don't emit the scents of expensive cologne or bath and body products. Instead, we give off the aroma of Christ. What must it smell like? Definitely better than fresh laundry, better than yeast bread baking, better than freshly mown grass, better than a baby just bathed, powdered, and dressed for bed. Far, far better.

I believe the aroma of Christ is akin to the presence of Christ. When inhaled fully, it overwhelms our senses and permeates dermis, bone, muscle, organ, and blood to reach that hidden place deep within the core of our being that is the soul.

Wonder if you've ever encountered the fragrance in another person? Tell me this: have you ever met someone about whom you said, "There's just something special about that person. I really can't put my finger on it, but whatever it is, I really like her." That, my friend, may just be the aroma of Christ.

Heaven Scent was the name of the first cologne set I purchased when I was thirteen. The packaging was powdery blue, bearing the silhouette of a cherub caught in midflight against a white background. Promoters describe the fragrance as "a fresh, beautiful, and enchanting floral bouquet with artistic undertones." My youthful opinion was simply that it smelled really good.

I was tempted to search online stores for a Heaven Scent product to see if my definition of "really good" has changed from fifty years ago. Of one thing I am certain: there is no man-made or natural scent or aroma that can match the compelling, overwhelming, and life-changing beauty of the true heavenly scent that is Christ Jesus.

Holy God, I am amazed at the exciting truths I continually discover within Your Word. Inspire me to dig deeper and to hunger for Your Word and Your wisdom to Your glory. Amen.

A Tender Heart Speaks

He will wipe all tears from their eyes, and there will be no more death, suffering, crying, or pain. These things of the past are gone forever.

—Revelation 21:4 (Contemporary English Version)

IN RECENT WEEKS, death passed close by. A former yoga student and friend passed, along with parents of several friends. I don't know about you, but each time I hear of someone losing her father, I flash back to the day in August 2001, when my own dad transitioned from this earthly life.

You see, I was a daddy's girl and had lived my whole life in dread of the day when he would take his last breath.

I was working out of town that first day of August. As was my habit, I'd called home the night before to let Mom and Dad know where I'd be, in case of emergency. The answering machine picked up, so I left a message. I later learned that Dad had been showering, and Mom had been helping a neighbor can green beans.

Work went smoothly that morning. My colleagues got word that Dad had passed during the night, but I wasn't told. As the afternoon session of court was about to begin, my boss beckoned me into his chambers. As I stepped through the door, I was bewildered when I saw my husband, Jim, and I said, "Honey, what are you doing here?" With tears in his eyes, he told me. The rest is a blur.

When I returned to work a week later, colleagues offered their condolences. But it was the reaction of one particular man that surprised and touched me deeply. He had been in the courtroom that day and knew that my husband was en route with the sad news. "I felt so sorry for you that day," he recounted. "I knew you didn't know yet, and it took me back to when I lost my own dad."

Let me say that I did not know this man well. He was a deputy US marshal, one of a dozen or more who also worked on the seventh floor. The US Marshals Service provides court security for the federal judges, transports federal prisoners to and from jail, and apprehends federal fugitives. I knew his name and would greet him formally on the rare occasions we passed in the hallway. To me, he was a stoic, serious federal lawman, devoid of emotions, with no time for unnecessary conversations.

But after that day, I saw him with new eyes.

He still looked the same. His appearance had not changed, except he may have been a tiny bit friendlier because of the conversation we'd had.

From that day forward, I knew that behind that stern countenance, behind the shiny marshal's badge, behind the dark suit and the furrowed brow, there was a man. Flesh and blood, not a caricature or a stereotype. And within that man there beats a heart that, like all of ours, will someday cease to beat. And that heart is tender and kind, feeling compassion and, yes, even empathy. And somewhere inside that man is a boy or young man who lost his father and still misses him.

I don't know anything about the man beyond what I have told

you here, except his first name is Wade. I can't remember his last name. I've not seen him since I retired and don't expect to ever see him again. But his reaching out to me taught me a lesson. Since then, I've understood that those of us who have lost loved ones have a heart connection to those who mourn. Unlike anyone whose life has yet to be personally touched by death, we have the precious gift of empathy. Having plodded through those slow, methodical steps of the grief journey, we understand the value of a hug, of holding a person's hand, of listening without comment, and of holding space for their pain.

The day will come when we will no longer lose family and friends, no longer weep and mourn, but, in the meantime, when we cast our eyes on other people, let us look beyond the outer person and recognize and honor the tender and often wounded hearts that lie within.

Lord, help us look beyond our fear of death and of saying the wrong thing to reach out to those who mourn, either by word or deed, to show that we care and that, above all else, that You care. Amen.

Fourteen Cans of Creamed Corn

For where your treasure is, there your heart will be also.

—Matthew 6:21 (King James Version)

MANY YEARS AGO, I was moving from one apartment to another, and my mom was helping. While I packed dishes, Mom was on her hands and knees in front of a cabinet, pulling out canned vegetables, sorting them, and packing them into boxes.

"Mercy, goodness!" she exclaimed.

I looked to see what she'd found.

"Fourteen cans of creamed corn?"

I smiled, slightly embarrassed. "I was afraid there would be a blizzard, and I couldn't get to the store."

She seemed dubious. "I didn't know you liked creamed corn."

Dropping my chin to my chest, I admitted, "I really don't, but it was on sale. Three cans for a dollar."

Mom just shook her head and went back to sorting.

Apparently, my initial purchase had been fifteen cans. Trust me when I say that if there were fourteen cans of creamed corn, there were also numerous cans of green beans, whole kernel corn, and peas. Who knows how many cans of vegetables I owned?

We've laughed about this through the years, Mom and I.

How is it that large quantities of "stuff" make us feel a sense of security?

Hoarding creamed corn was unusual for me. Toilet paper has been my thing for years. Long before the pandemic saw people swarming like bees every time store workers brought out a pallet of the fluffy white rolls, I always kept at least a month's worth on hand.

Isn't it funny how material things, even humble toilet tissue, can give us a sense of security?

Are there certain material things that give you a sense of security? How about a well-stocked refrigerator? A closet (or closets) full of clothes? A car? A full gas tank? Money in the bank? A comfortable and safe home? A generous supply of [fill in the blank]?

With COVID-19, life, as we knew it, came to a screeching halt. Confined to our homes with time on our hands, projects we'd never had time for finally got finished. There was so much decluttering happening in the first weeks of the pandemic, a friend and I agreed that charity stores would be overrun with inventory from all the donations pouring in, just from our own circle of friends. We Americans do like our stuff, don't we? If you're not careful, you may find yourself buying a bigger house or renting a storage space to accommodate it all.

Once the decluttering projects were over, we had plenty of time to think. Time to consider life. To look back on the past. Survey the present. Wonder about the future. Ask ourselves hard questions like: What is truly important? What doesn't matter as much as we'd thought? What should we keep? What do we need to let go?

Jesus didn't have a show on HGTV, but He does have advice regarding clutter. Jesus said the material "treasures" we accumulate here are temporary. He counsels us, "Do not store up for yourselves treasures on earth, where moths and vermin destroy, and where thieves break in and steal" (Matthew 6:19 New International Version).

What treasures can we store up that cannot be stolen or destroyed? Can you make a list?

When laboring over my own list, a light bulb came on. Christ must occupy the number-one spot. Otherwise, what is the purpose of my life? I am a weathered ship without a rudder, an exhausted traveler without a compass, a ragged bit of flotsam tossed about in the sea of existence.

Through the eyes of Christ, through His wisdom and His heart, we can distinguish treasures from temporal baubles. He nudges me when I get a little too preoccupied with the temporal and draws my focus back to things that really matter.

I opened a drawer yesterday and saw a tiny white cardboard box bearing my friend Mary Lee's name, written in ink—keepsakes her daughters had mailed me after Mary Lee's passing in December. Seeing the box reminded me that my forty-year friendship with Mary Lee is one of those treasures that Jesus spoke about. From laughter to tears, celebrations to heartaches, she and I weathered it all. Even though I miss her every day, death cannot diminish the joy and love in our relationship. It transcends time and space and will abide with me always.

Not so with the fourteen cans of creamed corn.

Lord, Your Word is timeless and Your truth all-powerful. Help me shake off all the extraneous clutter and focus on the true treasures in my life. Amen.

About Harold

> "The King will reply, 'Truly I tell you, whatever you did for one of the least of these brothers and sisters of mine, you did for me.'"
>
> —Matthew 25:40 (New International Version)

I MET HIM on a warm autumn evening in 1998. I'd left Jazzercise class early, hurrying out the doors with my gym bag over one shoulder and my purse over the other.

A street lamp cast a hazy, yellowish light on the narrow walkway leading to the normally deserted parking lot. But this particular evening was different.

Halfway between the church doors and my car, I was approached by an elderly gentleman, neatly dressed and well-groomed.

"Excuse me, ma'am," he said with pleading eyes. "Can you help me?"

Though I'd been in a rush, seeing this man so unexpectedly stopped me in my tracks. My momentary hesitation gave him just the opportunity he needed to tell me his story:

He needed money for a bus ticket. He had cancer. He was scheduled for treatment. His doctors were at the Veterans Hospital.

The hospital was fifty miles away. He had no way of getting there. He needed treatment. Did I have any money so he could get a bus ticket to make it to his appointment at the VA hospital?

As he spoke, he turned his pockets out to show me that he had neither money nor a weapon. He swore to me that he would not use the money for booze. He just had to get to the VA. He said his name was Harold.

Until he mentioned it, neither a weapon nor money for alcohol had entered my mind. Working in the court system, I saw people every week who carried weapons, and not one of them looked like Harold. When I looked into Harold's face, I was moved. Looking at him, I saw my dad, my uncle Frank, my uncle Don, my uncle Joe, my uncle Brooks, my uncle Harry—all navy veterans of World War II.

In the dim light, Harold appeared harmless. He couldn't have weighed more than 110 pounds soaking wet, and I was at least a head taller. How risky could this be?

Decisions, decisions.

I thought, *Lord, You're seeing this, right?*

I reached into the side pocket of my purse and pulled out my money. All I had was a twenty.

Aw, Lord! Do I have to give him an entire twenty?

Harold's eyes silently pleaded as I weighed my options.

I'm not certain, but I may have heard the God say, *You can't very well ask him for change, can you? His pockets are empty.*

I sighed. *All right, Lord.*

The decision was made, but I wasn't happy about it.

My voice was stern. "All right, Harold, let's go. I'm giving you all the money I have, *and* I'm taking you to the bus station."

Like a smiling leprechaun, Harold followed me to my car, hopped in, and buckled up.

The trip was a short one, maybe only ten blocks, but time enough for me to give Harold a lecture.

I am not proud of what I am about to share. As a matter of fact, I am, to this day, quite ashamed of my behavior. God knows my intention was good, but I felt fully justified in giving Harold the what-for.

Here's what I said: "Harold, you had better not be lying to me. I am trusting you, so you had better be telling me the truth."

"Oh, I am, I am," he promised, sounding like Floyd the barber from *The Andy Griffith Show.*

I heard coins clinking and glanced to my right. Harold had spied the loose change in the console.

"Here's some money," he said excitedly, stirring in the assortment of pennies, nickels, dimes, and quarters.

Oh, Lord!

When I pulled into the loading zone at the bus station, Harold was still digging through the coins and filling his once-empty pockets.

"Harold," I commanded, "you are *not* getting out of this car until I pray for you."

To say this was not one of my compassionate moments is a gross understatement.

But pray I did. Harold continued to stir the loose change as I prayed out loud for his health and for his protection. When I was finished, I don't know which of us was more relieved. Harold leaped out of the car, and I drove away, thinking, *My husband must never hear about this.*

The next day, a Wednesday, I met with my lunch-hour prayer group. Still in a state of mild shock, I told them about what had happened.

Margie chuckled and said, "So you met Harold, did you? He's

notorious for hanging around the churches over on the west side, begging money for alcohol."

My jaw dropped. My feathers fell. I had been duped. I felt like a deflated balloon. I'd risked my personal safety and handed over hard-earned money for what may have been a fictitious bus ticket to treat a nonexistent disease. I'd been conned.

My first reaction was embarrassment. Then anger. Then amusement. Once the dust settled, I was OK with it, knowing there was an underlying lesson.

For all I know, Harold may never have served in the military. What my eyes saw that night was a man in need. The years of living were etched in the lines of his face. Despite his downtrodden state, he was clean and neat. Habits he acquired in the military, perhaps. What I know for sure is that he was someone's son, father, brother, or uncle, reaching a hand out to a stranger.

What I felt was God telling me to give what I had; do what I could. A twenty-dollar bill, a ride, and a prayer.

Did Harold go directly to the liquor store with that twenty dollars? Maybe. Maybe not. It's not for me to speculate. My part in the story ended when Harold got out of the car. It was my test, not Harold's.

Since then, I've kept some small bills in the zipper side of my purse for the next time I run into a "Harold." I'll not seek him out, but if approached, I will hand the dollars over and kindly—with an emphasis on *kindly*—say, "God bless you, friend."

Lord, thank You for reminding me that I too could be Harold. Remind me to not take my many blessings for granted and to give with an open heart and open hands, for those who are in need may just be Jesus in disguise. Amen.

The Legacy of Mama

Her children arise and call her blessed; her husband also, and he praises her: "Many women do noble things, but you surpass them all." Charm is deceptive, and beauty is fleeting; but a woman who fears the Lord is to be praised.

—Proverbs 31:28–30 (New International Version)

JULIA AND SUSAN think about their mama every day.

I never met Mama, but from the daughters she raised, I know she was an exceptional woman. A Proverbs 31 kind of woman. I see the values Mama instilled in her girls, the tender hearts that she gently nurtured, and the humble confidence she infused with her steadfast love.

Their sunny, welcoming smiles draw others to them, like metal to magnets. It's just who they are. It's their nature to open their arms to encompass people, even beyond friends and family, from premature infants in the Neonatal Intensive Care Unit to adults learning English as a second language.

Mama hailed from Kentucky, on the edge of horse country, with its rolling bluegrass meadows. I've known several people from Kentucky, all good and decent folk. I feel a kinship with

Julia and Susan, as our ancestors were separated only by the expanse of the Ohio River.

As I said, I never met Mama, but I know her through her legacy, her daughters.

During the pandemic, I thought often of my parents and my grandparents, and of the hardships my grandmothers endured during their lives.

Alone at age sixteen, my paternal grandmother, Mary, traveled alone from Poland to come live with her aunt in the United States.

Becky, my maternal grandmother, left school at age ten, when her mother died. As the only daughter, Grandma Becky assumed the care of her two younger brothers, in addition to running the household, until her father remarried some six years later.

Granny Mary wed a young hardworking Polish coal miner. Together, they raised four boys and four girls and cared for a disabled grandson in a small company house in a mining town in a deep Appalachian valley. Her kitchen was filled with the scents of fresh-baked bread, coffee, and something hearty simmering in a pot on the back of the stove. Her children adored her, their *matka*.

At nineteen, shy Grandma Becky married a charming store clerk ten years her senior. She bore thirteen children. Their ninety-acre farm fed the family, and Becky's skills as a seamstress brought in extra money. As years passed, every weekend, her home was full of laughter, with every bed full and children sleeping on the floor, since no one ever passed up a chance to come home to visit Mom.

On days when I am whiney, when I think I cannot stand another day of whatever minor inconvenience I'm experiencing, I remember my grandmothers. They never complained. Not once.

They took pleasure in simple things—sitting on the front porch swing after the supper dishes were done. Afternoon soap operas. Feeding family and strangers, regardless of the time of day or night. Serving bread and butter and coffee milk to the grandchildren. *Saturday Night Wrestling* from WOAY-TV in Oak Hill. A new housedress. A new apron. Folks dropping by for a visit.

When I am feeling particularly challenged and not up to the task, I remember Granny and Grandma and remind myself that theirs is the blood that runs through my veins. I am the legacy of these tough yet kind, determined women, so I straighten up and stand a little taller.

"Remember who you are," my friend Sarah's father used to tell his children. Good, solid, sound advice. We are not disconnected, solo artists, living in a universe of one. We are integral parts of something much greater than ourselves. We are family. We are community. We are citizens of the world.

As Christ followers, we also remind ourselves whose we are. To whom do we belong? Created in His image, we all carry God's DNA. Have you ever considered that? Look at your hand, your arm, your finger, and think about it. God's DNA is within you and me. Once I came to that realization, I never looked at my body in the same way again.

Some people might never have known their grandparents or even their parents, but we do know the one we traditionally refer to as our heavenly Father. God is called by many names—Mother, Father, the Almighty, the Divine, the Great I Am, Yahweh—yet no single name has ever captured the length, breadth, and depth of God's divine nature or His immeasurable love for us.

Just like Julia and Susan are Mama's legacy, they are also God's legacy, as are we. We were created for a time such as this—to stand tall, to shake off the cultural fallout, and to remember who we are and whose we are, so the divinity within us can shine forth and light the way forward.

Heavenly and holy God, You send people like Julia and Susan into my life to inspire me. Thank You for that and for every person whose life intersects with mine. Bind us together with Your love and encouragement, that others will see from whence our strength comes. Amen.

I Couldn't Believe My Eyes

For just as the body is one and has many members, and all the members of the body, though many, are one body, so it is with Christ.

—2 Corinthians 12:12 (English Standard Version)

IT WAS MID-NOVEMBER, chilly and damp in the mid-Atlantic states. Misty rain threatened to turn to snow at any moment.

Our Saturday morning ritual was to leave the farm early for the half-hour drive to town. Our first stop was a locally owned drive-through coffee shop. From there, we ran errands, including the grocery, before ending with lunch out.

In between stops, we shared details of our workweek. Jim described building a road as a courtesy to a group just outside town. I was unfamiliar with the group and the area, even though it was within an hour's drive of our farm.

Our last stop was Lowe's. Jim was oblivious to the weather, since he spent so much time out in the elements. I, on the other hand, pulled up my hood and clutched my coat tightly to my throat as we hurried across the parking lot. We were on a mission for supplies. No dawdling allowed. Daylight was burning and, if you are familiar with farming, you know chores always await.

Lowe's was decked out for Christmas. Like a kid in a candy store, my head involuntarily swiveled right to left, taking in the sparkly decorations, while keeping up with Jim's purposeful gait. I could picture that wreath on the back door, that garland across the entry way—hold the phone! No amount of glitter or shine could distract me from what I saw coming toward us in the main aisle of the store.

Approaching were two men in floor-length black cassocks. The toes of muddy boots peeked out with each step. Their frizzy, untamed beards hung nearly to their waists. Hand-carved, wooden pectoral crosses on rough ropes swayed to and fro with each step. Black brimless caps, matching their cassocks, topped their heads, and their long, flowing hair was caught up into low ponytails.

It's not polite to stare, so I was doing the glance, ook away, glance, lookaway thing as we rapidly approached them. This apparition appeared so quickly that there wasn't time for me to poke my husband in the ribs and say, "Look!" before the strangest thing of all happened.

When they were within ten feet of us, the younger of the two opened his mouth and spoke.

"Hey, Jim. How're you doing?"

They stopped. We stopped. I stared.

"Hey, Father Alexander, I'm doing fine."

A short conversation ensued. To me, it sounded something like, "thisismywifebeckythisisfathersoandsonicetomeetyou ivebeentellingheraboutthesoapyoumake …" In other words, my brain was having a hard time processing what I was seeing and hearing. Was I dreaming or had I stepped through a portal into the Twilight Zone right in the midst of Lowe's center aisle?

I would later learn these men were from the Holy Cross

Monastery, an English-speaking monastery of the Russian Orthodox Church, and my husband knew them. He had built a road for them the prior week. Their website describes the property as 180 acres "in the beautiful foothills of the Appalachian Mountains. The surrounding hills and forests provide the monastery with seclusion from the distractions and temptations of the world, as well as a daily reminder of the beauty of God's creation."

That day, I could not fathom that there was a Russian Orthodox monastery so close by, that anyone would want to live that way, and that these men were real flesh-and-blood people who shopped at Lowe's on Saturday morning.

Now, twenty-odd years later, joy bubbles up in me as I think about these men living a life separate and dedicating themselves to honoring God with their prayer, worship, labor, and community living. Some have been with the community for many years. Some are new. All have a common purpose in mind.

God is so amazing, isn't He? He knows when to challenge us and when to let us tread water. He keeps us in one place for a season; then He whispers, "Trust me," as He leads us into what for us is uncharted territory.

God is not going to press me into a mold to fit someone else's idea of what a Christian looks like. His work cannot be accomplished if we all want to drive the truck or if we all want to follow instead of lead.

In considering the relative isolation and the hard physical labor in all seasons and all weather, one might think one could never live like that. *Me either*, I think. At least not for long, but God hasn't asked me to. If He ever does, we'll cross that bridge then—God and me. Because He won't ask me to do anything that He does not first equip me to do.

I never saw those fellows again, but the image of their

appearance that day will never leave me. The very next week, when Jim returned to finish up the road project, the brothers expressed their gratitude and blessed him with a gift basket of their own goat's milk soap, made from the milk of their resident goats, of course.

Lord, You have a job for us all to do. Remind us that we are all one in Your kingdom, now and forever. Amen.

Alone

After sending the people away, He went up a hill by himself to pray. When evening came Jesus was there alone.

—Matthew 14:23 (Good News Translation)

ALONE.

Just saying the word stirs the emotions. Prior to the outbreak of COVID-19, we were conditioned to think of *alone* as being either positive or negative. More than a year into the pandemic, our opinions may have changed.

Jesus knew the value of being alone. Each time He stepped away from the disciples or the crowds that followed Him, He was having His alone time with God—a time to be refreshed and replenished.

During those times, I believe Jesus was listening to and conversing with God. His opening statement could well have been, "Oh, Lord, what a day I have had," as He proceeded to share the day's events with Father God. Never once did God interrupt, saying impatiently, "I already know everything that happened today." Not once. And if Jesus had hesitated with, "You really don't want to hear this," then God would have eagerly responded, "Yes, I do. I want to hear absolutely everything. Talk to Me, Son." Relieved, Jesus would continue to speak, as His tired body relaxed and peace settled over His heart and soul.

For us to live life fully, embracing the abundance offered, we need alone time with God, either planned or spontaneous. Early morning alone time can make all the difference in how you view circumstances that arise during your day. It needn't be complicated and can be as simple as sitting quietly, undistracted, and thinking about God.

Recently, I found myself awake at 3:00 a.m., with no hope of going back to sleep. Hoping not to awaken the rest of the house, I tiptoed from the bedroom and headed for the sofa. Sleep continued to elude me, but I had two choices: let my thoughts run wild in a thousand different directions, or use the time to think about God. I chose the latter.

Curled up under a fuzzy blanket, I reminded myself of God's protective stronghold over our lives, of His tender mercies, of His extravagant blessings and His promises to never leave or forsake us. It's impossible not to relax when you allow yourself to rest in God. I recalled Psalm 91:4 from the Living Bible: "He will shield you with His wings! They will shelter you. His faithful promises are your armor." Before long, the soft blanket began to feel like downy feathers of God's mighty wings, and I fell asleep, smiling.

I hope the next time you find yourself alone—whether in a hospital bed or on a beach, in the middle of the day or the middle of the night—you won't allow your thoughts to run amok. Take control of your thoughts by focusing on God. Pray, even if it is as simple a prayer as, "Lord, help." Sing a song. Read or recite scripture. Our God hears it all. He is right there, as close as the breath you breathe.

Lord, the middle of the night can be a dark and lonely place. Thank You for reminding us that You are always there. We can rest well, knowing You are keeping watch. Thank You for teaching me new lessons each day. I love You with my whole heart. Amen.

A Gift of Bread

While they were eating, Jesus took the bread, and
when He had given thanks, He broke it and gave it
to His disciples, saying, "Take, eat; this is my body."

—Matthew 26:26 (New International Version)

THE PACKAGE ARRIVED promptly. Rectangular in form,
shaped like a shoe box, it had traveled through the US mail all the
way to Florida from my cousin Dawne in Maryland.

When I laid eyes on it, my saliva glands kicked into overdrive
because I knew what was inside. Nut roll made from my Polish
grandmother's recipe.

The stubborn packing tape was no deterrent, and like a person
starved, I sliced the box open with a paring knife. With one swift
movement, I pulled out the roll and placed it unceremoniously
on the cutting board. When I grabbed the big chef's knife, my
curious husband took a step or two backward. I shoved aside the
layers of foil and plastic wrap, split the loaf in half and then, with
another deft flick of the wrist, I cut myself a thick slab.

It felt like slow motion. Using both hands, I lifted the slice of nut-filled delight to my mouth and took a bite. With eyes closed, I chewed slowly and sighed. "Granny!"

As far as appearance and texture go, Granny's nut roll (also known as *kolache*) is no food stylist's dream. The loaf is lumpy and uneven, and the few times I've made it, it was dry even when fresh. It may be a little too brown in spots or cracked where the delectable, sweet walnut filling leaks out. No matter. Granny made it with love, and she only made it at Christmastime. Each of her eight children received a loaf. It was a highlight of our family holiday.

So cousin Dawne honored the memory of our grandmother, not only by making Granny's nut roll but by sharing it with me. Every bite I took transported me back to Granny's kitchen. Nowadays, we show hospitality by offering a visitor something to drink—coffee, tea, soda—but Granny, in her thick Polish accent, would always say, "You wan' some-ting to eat?" She wanted to make sure no one was ever hungry. I wonder if that wasn't because she herself had known hunger as a child in Poland.

She left us with wonderful memories of her yeast rolls, homemade raised doughnuts, pierogi, biscuits, and cornbread.

Bread, in every form, is the most basic form of human sustenance.

Making bread is an act of love, as is the breaking of bread and sharing it—with friends, family, and strangers.

Jesus may not have baked the bread eaten at the Last Supper, but with His own hands, He shared it. With His own hands, He broke the bread in order to serve it to His disciples. The loaf could not have been shared without first being broken, just as Jesus could not offer Himself as salvation for the world without literally being broken.

Jesus accepted His fate "for the forgiveness of sins" (Matthew 26:28, New International Version) for all of humankind. He who was blameless took the blame for us all. He who was whole became broken for us.

Back to the nut roll: later that day, I called my cousin to tell her it had arrived safely and to thank her.

"Oh, Dawne, I have to tell you. When I took that first bite, all I could say was, 'Granny!'"

I could hear her smiling. "You could not have given me any greater compliment."

I smiled back. It was my pleasure!

Lord, thank You for stirring good memories; thank You for friends and family with whom I can share them and especially for the sacrifice of Jesus, our Savior, the true Bread of Life. Amen.

The Chicken Speaks

Then the LORD opened the donkey's mouth, and it said to Balaam, "What have I done to you to make you beat me these three times?"

—Numbers 22:28 (New International Version)

THE CHICKENS SPOKE among themselves in low, conspiratorial tones as my niece Quincy and I walked slowly up the slight incline from the creek bed. Peering at us with interest, heads cocked to the side, eleven Rhode Island Red hens moved cautiously toward us, interested yet ready to bolt at any moment.

I recalled being pecked by a hen as a nine-year-old, gathering eggs at Aunt Dott's farm. The problem, I now know, was that I was reaching into the nest before the hen was finished laying her eggs. No wonder she pecked me!

"You want to hold one?" Quincy asked.

Before I could answer, my free-spirited niece bent down, scooped up the nearest hen, and offered her to me. The rest of "the girls" scattered in all directions.

I'd never held a hen, and I wasn't about to start while wearing a jacket I'd borrowed from my sister-in-law, so I declined, but

I watched with interest as Quincy tucked her feathered friend under her arm and began stroking those deep auburn feathers, crooning to her in soothing tones just above a whisper.

I looked on in wonder.

"Do you want to pet her?" she asked.

Mesmerized, I nodded and extended my hand but kept it well back from that pointy little beak, just in case.

This was new for me. I've petted my share of cats, dogs, rabbits, guinea pigs, hamsters, horses, a cow, several calves, and even a pig but never a bird.

The feathers felt just like they looked, so sleek, silky, and shiny that they almost appeared wet. With long, even strokes, I ran my hand from the back of her neck, down over her back to her tail. From all appearances, Mrs. Hen enjoyed being petted.

"Feel this." My niece touched the hen's comb, that strange appendage that grows up the center of their foreheads from their beaks to where their eyebrows would be, if hens had eyebrows.

Following her lead, I used my index finger and thumb to explore the leathery texture of her brilliant crimson comb. The hen did not protest.

"Did you know that the color of their earlobes indicates what color eggs they lay?"

I did not know that.

"Do you want to see her ear?"

I nodded.

With the tips of her fingers, my niece gentled parted the tuft of feathers on the side of the hen's head to reveal a round opening the size of the tip of a ballpoint pen. A chicken's ear! I was fascinated.

Mindlessly, I continued to pet the hen, but what I felt next took me aback. With the very next stroke I made down her feathery back, I did something that I always do with a dog or a cat or any other beast I have ever petted. I buried my fingers into her feathers to give her skin a good scratch.

Instead of feeling soft, supple skin, it felt like I'd stuck my fingers into a network of toothpicks—dry and brittle and unyielding. Unbeknownst to me, hidden beneath the silky-smooth feather tips are the stiff and sturdy quills, the bare part of the feather that attaches to the skin of the bird.

I was shocked! My sensory system was expecting smooth, silky feathers leading all the way down to soft chicken skin, not this bristly, dry, what-is-*that*? sensation.

"Oooh." My eyebrows shot up.

Quincy smiled. "Weird, huh?"

"Weird," I agreed, forcing a smile. I didn't recoil, but I wanted to. It wasn't particularly unpleasant, just unexpected. Different, but good.

Life is full of episodes like that—when we are expecting one thing and, instead, get something else. But that's not necessarily a bad thing, even if, at first, we are disappointed or sad or shocked or even angry. Our egos convince us how things should be, what will make us happy, or what a perfect world looks like, but God usually has other plans. Better plans—often, plans that are so much better that they are beyond our wildest imaginings or plans we never would have dared to dream.

As believers, we embrace Romans 8:28: "God works *all* things together for good for the ones who love God, for those who are called according to His purpose" (Common English Bible). Our part is so easy. We just have to love Him, and He works out everything else.

Can you think of a time in your life when you were expecting one thing and what you actually got was different but better?

Can you think of a time when God used your painful

experience to help someone else going through the same hard time?

When I love God, He turns my scars into stars, my failures into accomplishments, and my messes into messages. When we love God, He can teach us.

The red hen spoke to me that day without ever moving her beak. Without words, she delivered God's message, loud and clear. It's a message I never grow weary of hearing.

The chicken said, "God works *all* things—not some, not a couple, but *all* things—together for good for those who love Him. Just trust Him. Seek His voice. Rest on His promises. Stand on His Word."

Message delivered. She blinked her little chicken eye and looked away. If I hadn't still been nervous about her beak, I could've kissed her.

Great God, thank You for all Your creatures. Thank you for Your holy Word. Lead me to look for You in all Your creation and listen for Your voice each and every day so that I might love You with all that I am. Amen.

Ministers with Paws

Then God commanded, "Let the earth produce all kinds of animal life: domestic and wild, large and small"—and it was done. So God made them all, and He was pleased with what He saw. Then God said, "And now we will make human beings."

—Genesis 1:24–26 (Good News Translation)

I GREW UP on a small farm. Moving to my husband's farm seemed a smooth transition, except for one slight wrinkle. In my family of origin, animals lived outside, and people lived inside.

My first order of business, as lady of the manor, was to promptly usher three sixty-pound dogs off the living room furniture, out of the house, and into the barn. My husband must have been blinded by love to tolerate my behavior, as I soon realized I had married into a family of animal lovers.

As a part of my new family, I've seen orphaned baby rabbits and newborn kittens fed with eyedroppers and abandoned puppies coaxed out of a hollow tree on a rainy winter night. In order to accommodate his feeding schedule, a baby squirrel that had fallen from his treetop nest was a special guest one year at our big family Christmas dinner. When they were old enough, the rabbits and squirrel were returned to the wild, and the puppies and kittens found homes with family or friends.

This love of animals was quite foreign to me. I'd always thought you either like animals or you don't. Although I'd always been a cat owner, dogs weren't my thing. Too boisterous, too demanding, too in your face with the hot, smelly breath. Then, I spent time with Echo.

Echo was one of the three dogs I'd booted out, but it wasn't long before she won my heart. Even now, she shares the title of the sweetest dog ever. Her wavy coat was as black as ebony. Appearance-wise, she resembled the herding breed Bouvier des Flandres and had the people-pleasing temperament of a golden retriever. Undemanding. Affectionate. Happy.

Echo had beautiful eyes, a rich brown with dark flecks, giving them great depth and dimension. When I gazed into her eyes, I felt a deep connection, like she was my best friend, my soul sister. Because of Echo, I too became an animal lover.

When I went for long walks on the farm, Echo went with me. A quarter mile from the farmhouse stood a boulder I named my prayer rock. Any time I walked that path, I would scale the prayer rock and sit a while, my face turned upward, gazing at the tall trees that surrounded the path. I watched the leaves flutter in the breeze and the sun intermittently peek through the branches. I closed my eyes against the light and inhaled the rich, loamy scents of the forest floor. My ears were attuned to the subtle movements of the woodland creatures—chipmunks, squirrels, birds, a distant flock of wild turkeys, even insects.

Beside me on the prayer rock, Echo snuggled into my side, panting. I scratched her head. As soon as I stopped scratching, she nuzzled my hand, wanting more.

A funny thing happened one morning in late summer. Echo was beside me, and I was praying aloud, with only God, Echo, and the trees to hear me. When I said, "Thank you, God, for the blessing of our animals," Echo stopped panting and went silent, as if to pay homage to the holiness of the moment. I smiled and planted a kiss on her furry head.

Researchers tell us that petting an animal reduces our stress and anxiety, lowers blood pressure, and combats depression. Owning a dog can encourage regular exercise and social interaction. If you want to meet your neighbors, walk a dog.

Therapy dogs are showing up everywhere, in places like hospitals, assisted-care facilities, schools, libraries, and courtrooms. Petting a dog can take one's mind off pain, calm the nerves, and make an unfamiliar setting a little less intimidating.

Dogs are like ministers with paws; clergy wrapped in fur. They listen without judging. They are gentle. They are honest (a dog's tail never lies). Dogs are always there for you, regardless of the day or the hour, and they often make you laugh. They encourage good health, insisting you take them out, rain or shine, for a breath of fresh air. Dogs sense when you need a cuddle and demand little in exchange for all that they give. They are a true gift from God.

Take another look at the creation story in Genesis 1. I am inclined to think that, in between verses 25 and 26, God had a lengthy and detailed conversation with the dogs about the ins and outs of their earthly assignment as "man's best friend."

And then came the moment for which the entire canine population had been waiting. Picture it: eyes wide, ears alert, waiting and watching for the arrival of Adam and Eve.

At long last, they appear, man and woman, dogs' best friends!

A cacophony of yipping, barking, tail wagging, circle running, and romping erupted, the likes of which has never been repeated in the history of the world. The joyful sounds echoed from the mountains to the deserts to the sea.

And God saw that it was good. *Really* good.

Lord, thank You for the gift of pets. They embody Your unconditional love. They teach us patience and kindness and, at times, sacrifice. For that, we give thanks. Amen.

God Bless Teachers

Children are a gift from the Lord; they are a real blessing.

—Psalm 127:3 (Good New Translation)

EACH SUMMER, MY friend Cassie and her husband spend the better part of June at a beach rental, unwinding, relaxing, and getting away from everyday life for a while before school recommences in August. And she deserves it. Cassie teaches second grade; she has for years.

Her current assignment is at a public elementary in the poorest of neighborhoods. In the years we've known each other, Cassie has, at times, expressed feeling both frustrated and disheartened by the public school environment, yet when asked why she continues to teach, even though she has more than enough years in to retire, she always gives the same answer with a gentle smile: "Because I love the children."

Last year, I noticed something different about her. There was a subtle but definite change, but I just couldn't put my finger on it. Curious, I asked if something had changed in her life. Yes, indeed, she said. At work. A personnel shift had brought new leadership to her school. With it came new routines, new attitudes, and an enthusiasm for learning that swept through the school like a tidal wave.

A smile illuminated her face, and her eyes sparkled. "It's such a great environment now." The teachers had a heart for the students and for their coworkers, and the children could feel it. Even the most recalcitrant students were caught up in the new creative energy. Plus, the teachers and staff had a secret weapon. "We pray," Cassie said, her voice softening. "Before each school day begins, we pray for the students, and we pray for each other." Secret weapon, indeed!

And God knows these children, living on the edge, need divine intervention. Prior to the altered school schedules brought on by COVID-19, the children could always count on the school being open and their teachers being present. They could rely on being allowed inside, out of the elements, and being fed a healthy breakfast and lunch. That's important to the little boy who lives with his dad at the city mission and to children from single-parent or tumultuous homes. And don't forget the kids whose parents share custody. The children and their teachers must keep track of which bus they are to take on which day to go to home, or to the noncustodial parent, or to Grandma's house.

So I say, God bless teachers. They are a stabilizing force for all children. They teach, they inspire, they model, and they protect with open hands and open hearts.

As for my friend Cassie, she celebrated her sixty-fifth birthday last week, but that hasn't slowed her down or dampened her enthusiasm one bit. She continues to look forward to another new school year and the opportunity to make a difference in the world, one student at a time.

"As long as I feel like what I am doing makes a difference, I'll continue to teach," she said. Her full, rich voice is easy on the ears, and I imagined how comforting it must be to listen to her read to her class.

I smiled at her. "Your students are very lucky to have you as a teacher," I said. "You are one of those they'll remember their entire lives."

With humility and grace, she smiled and said, "You're sweet. Thank you."

Lord, lay Your hand on all those who dedicate themselves to teaching. Assure them in their hearts that they truly do make a positive impact on the world, and give them courage, comfort, encouragement, and strength. Amen.

Dust Bunnies

If we confess our sins, He is faithful and just and
will forgive us our sins and purify us from all our
unrighteousness.

—1 John 1:9 (King James Version)

TWO THINGS THAT make me smile are early morning sunshine and clean, shiny floors. I'll be the first to admit, however, that when I am in charge of housekeeping, the sun shines much more often than our floors. Oyster is the color of our tile. Attractive, yes, but hard to keep clean. Every little speck shows. When you share the house with two "children with fur" (dogs) and have a casual relationship with the vacuum, you may have dust and specks and twigs and bits of grass and mulch. The dust and the fur eventually combine to create dust bunnies.

Dust bunnies are those ethereal and elusive little bits of fluff that always seem to appear, just when you've settled your guests onto the sofa for a pleasant visit.

Think fast, and you can divert your guests' attention temporarily, but it would seem that dust bunnies have minds of their own. They will twirl and spin, and, if you're lucky, they will wrap themselves around a table leg or skid to a stop on the edge of a rug before your guests notice.

A household record was set last week when, under my bed, I discovered a dust bunny the size of a ten-week-old kitten. Most people might be too embarrassed to admit it, but I am both fascinated, impressed, and, apparently, shameless.

All my life, housecleaning has been a huge production for me. Lately, I've tried to adopt the mantra, "Leave the room tidier than when you arrived." That worked for a while, but my normal cleaning style is knock-down, drag-out cleaning—everyone out of the house, and stay out; clear the decks; here I come; all or nothing. When the job is complete, the results are so worth it. If it could only stay that way, right?

A sparkling-clean house reminds me of how I feel after I've come clean with God and confessed my sins. I may think I can do a little surface cleaning, minimizing my sin or simply denying it altogether, but that's like shoving the mess into a closet and quickly closing the door (which, by the way, I have done). Eventually, the latch will give way, or someone will innocently open that closet door, and the entire mess will come tumbling out.

Why are we hesitant to confess to God? Is it because we imagine God in human terms, as a disappointed parent, a strict disciplinarian, or an impossible-to-please boss? It's easy to do; people are people, and God is God. I believe we can trust God to never treat us harshly. God will never overreact, criticize, dramatize, or lecture. God's ways are much higher than our ways. God knows us so well that, long before it ever occurred, He knew we were going to sin. It's the nature of humans. Fortunately for us, it is the nature of our benevolent and compassionate God to welcome us, tear-stained and bearing the grime and stench of the world, into His all-encompassing arms. He is not disgusted. Quite the contrary. God is delighted when we approach the throne of grace, seeking forgiveness. God reaches for us and soothes us. The cleansing power of our heavenly Father is tender yet effective. He restores and renews us. Like a recently cleaned house, our hearts and souls are refreshed. And all we need to do is confess and ask for His forgiveness.

Sin, like dust bunnies, will show up again and again. That's life. But if we make a regular practice of seeking God's forgiveness, we'll never have to worry about what's behind those closet doors or beneath our beds.

Holy and gracious God, help me make a daily practice of confessing my sin to You. Reveal to me my unknown sin. Let me honor Your great love by obeying Your commands. Amen.

Big Mouth, Big Foot

So I always take pains to have a clear conscience
toward both God and man.

—Acts 24:16 (English Standard Version)

WHAT DO YOU remember about elementary school? I remember the gritty sensation of the blackboard chalk on my fingers and in my nose; the fetid odor of the rough, brown paper towels when wet; and having to repeatedly line up for lunch, recess, or the bus.

One day, we were told to line up along the blackboard for a math lesson on measurements. We were about to learn that the twelve-inch ruler was not merely a weapon for fending off pesky brothers or drawing straight lines on paper.

To demonstrate the proper use of a ruler, an exercise was conducted. The teacher wrote each student's name on the board and separated us into pairs. Using our rulers, we were to measure each other's smile and record the results on the board. Once the measurements were posted, we all stood back to read the results.

It may have been by only a fraction of an inch, but my smile (mouth) measured the broadest in my class. I was pleased. Little did I know then that my mouth would, on many, many occasions, need to accommodate an equally large foot.

There are times I have regretted *not* saying something, like "I love you," "thank you," or "I'm sorry." But I couldn't begin to count the times I wish I'd kept my big mouth shut—times I have blathered on boringly or tried to make a joke that came out as inappropriate. Times I've given advice when only a sympathetic ear was needed. And, yes, I've even traded insult for insult, long past the days of childish taunts like "I know you are, so what am I?"

Lord, have mercy.

In the wake of words misspoken, I can only remind myself that I am God's creation. Although He would not will me to insult, He's not surprised by my words or my deeds.

After much self-chastening, I prayerfully ponder the appropriate remedy for my offending words. Is an apology in order, or should I leave well enough alone?

Have you ever apologized to someone you carelessly insulted, only to have her respond, "No, I was not offended"? You may feel a bit strange, at first, when you hear the response. But how much better you will feel afterward and how treasured the other person will feel, knowing you cared enough about her feelings to speak up.

Often, I hear the words of Psalm 19:14—"Let the words of my mouth and the meditation of my heart be acceptable in Thy sight, O Lord, my Strength and my Redeemer" (Twenty-First Century King James Version). In all sincerity and with my whole heart, I pray it be so!

Lord, I present myself to You, warts and all, and You love me as Your favorite child. Forgive my sins and teach me Your ways. Amen.

Christmas Hope

The Word became flesh and made His dwelling among us. We have seen His glory, the glory of the One and Only Son, Who came from the Father, full of grace and truth.

—John 1:14 (English Standard Version)

THE SPIRITUAL HOPE of the Christmas season is indescribable. As we surrender to the anticipation of the arrival of the Christ child, we are moved. The soul stirs. The pulse quickens. Hearts are soothed by this powerful unguent.

Like a perfect gift, we receive it year after year. Knowing the storyline makes it all the sweeter. We wrap ourselves in the cloak of the eternal.

Yet we know there is another side to the Christmas season.

At this tender time of the year, we sense loss more keenly.

You see the chair at the dinner table, empty now because a young life was tragically cut short.

You go to share news with a friend and remember there's no one there to answer.

Lost dreams, lost relationships.

Loneliness echoes down empty hallways.

In the midst of our pain, we imagine that everyone else is celebrating in the style of a Norman Rockwell illustration. From my reading, Norman Rockwell's life was not what was portrayed in his art. He was divorced early on, married again but was widowed suddenly, and, along with his third wife, suffered depression most of his life. Perhaps he too yearned for the life he so magically created on canvas.

The spiritual hope of Christmas keeps us, above all else, focused on the eastern sky. We appreciate but are not distracted by pine trees, twinkling lights, bright ribbons, and rustling tissue paper. When all is said and done, the last pine needles are swept out, and the lights are stored away for yet another year, but our hope remains.

Join me in embracing the hope that connects us to the eternal Father, and experience that the holy gift only grows sweeter with the passage of time.

Lord, the twinkling Christmas tree lights remind us that Christ is the light in the darkness. Let us draw from that eternal hope to look beyond ourselves and to You. Amen.

Forgive Me, Mr. NFL

And forgive us our debts, as we forgive our debtors.
—Matthew 6:12 (King James Version)

THE ART OF letter writing may have gone by the wayside, but I still enjoy writing them, receiving them, and discovering old ones in a random box of papers. You may find the contents of the letter I share to be odd. Sometimes, we are unaware of little sins, those everyone-does-it kind of sins, until, from time to time, God gently but effectively brings them to our attention. It's how we learn and grow on this faith journey of ours. Although I never mailed the following letter, the simple act of writing it proved cathartic. I learned my lesson well. Here it is:

Dear Mr. NFL,

I have an apology to make. Monday morning, when I heard the score of Sunday's play-off game and that your team had lost, I said an enthusiastic, "Good!" Immediately, I felt ashamed, as if God had flicked me on the ear to get my attention. Ouch!

You see, lately I've been pondering how the world always latches onto and remembers the worst thing a person ever did. You read it in the news all the time. If you commit a crime, you are always a criminal. No amount of subsequent good behavior will erase the stain. Even if not convicted, accusations and innuendo often follow public figures doggedly.

So I gloated over your team's defeat because of the malice I held in my heart for you, Mr. NFL. Why did I feel that way? After all, I've never met you. I've only seen you on TV. I based my attitude solely on claims that, on several occasions before you married, you assaulted women. True or not, I personally judged and convicted you, locked you up, and threw away the key.

And on that Monday morning, when God got my attention, I was filled with remorse. What should I do? I wondered.

The Bible had the answer for me in the sixth chapter of Matthew. When offering up the Lord's Prayer, we ask God to "forgive us our trespasses as we forgive those who trespass against us." Speaking for myself, I want God to forgive and forget, as in Psalm 103, where God removes our sin "as far as the east is from the west," flinging it out into nothingness, never to be heard from or mentioned again. So, Mr. NFL, how dare I pray to be forgiven myself when I harbor judgment in my heart against you? How dare I?

I am writing to confess my sin against you and to seek forgiveness from you and from God. I realize it may not be a big deal to you, since you don't even know me, but I believe that God desires it of me.

Being in the public eye, you are an easy target. Some even say it comes with the territory. But gloating does not become me. Nor does taunting. I have sinned against you. Even though you seem larger than life, you are flesh and blood, just like the rest of us. We were both created by God. God loves you just as much as He loves me. The attitude I displayed toward you is one of those "little foxes that spoil the vines" of my joy and peace. I am thankful that God brought it to my attention. I offer you this heartfelt apology for my behavior.

Forgiving, as you may know, is not easy. I would like to think that you will consider my plea and offer your forgiveness, but if you choose not to, I am content with that. I feel better already, just for having gotten it off my chest.

Thank for taking the time to read this.

All my best to your wife and children.

Lord, thank You for poking me, "flicking me on the ear," and tugging on my heartstrings when I need it. It is easy to get caught up in attitudes and opinions that swirl around us and to forget who we are. Help me, Lord, to be as lavish with my love of others as You are with Yours. Amen.

Avoiding the Mirror

Search me, O God, and know my heart; try me and
know my thoughts. And see if there be any wicked
way in me, and lead me in the way everlasting.

—Psalm 139:23–24 (King James Version)

MY APPOINTMENT WITH the dermatologist rolls around
once a year, at which I'm examined from top to bottom and even
between the toes as the doctor checks for suspicious-looking
freckles and moles. In between appointments, experts say we
should do self-exams and be on the lookout for areas of concern.

We rely on doctors to conduct our physical exams, but what
about a spiritual exam? Do I make spiritual self-examination a
regular practice? No, I do not. My natural inclination is to shy
away from looking at myself too closely for fear I might spiral
downward, preoccupied with flaws that, perhaps, only I can see.

The good news is that we can trust God to do the job for us in
a gentle, loving way. We don't even have to formulate the prayer
because the psalmist has done the work for us. When we trust in
God, we can put it all out there, unafraid and unashamed.

So we pray—with all sincerity, heart, mind, and spirit—"Search me, God. Point out my errors, and cleanse my thoughts so my words do not offend." God will answer and reveal to us our sinful attitudes, thoughts, and behaviors.

You may be shocked by what you learn. The truth is never pretty. Facing it can be tough. When God kindly confronts me, how ashamed I am! How could I not have known? What damage have I done? I am filled with remorse. My heart breaks, but God Himself applies the unguent to ease my pain and heal my wound.

I sometimes picture myself before almighty God. He is vast, and I am small, reduced to a six-year-old, head hung low, avoiding eye contact, with chocolate-smeared lips and a red face, asking, "What stolen chocolate bar?"

Take comfort with me in the knowledge that God has heard it all before. Nothing—not one thing—surprises God. Let's drop the pretense and "become as little children" (Matthew 18:2–4 NIV).

Picture it, won't you? He is vast, and we are small. Come as you are. No need to be shy. This isn't a bait-and-switch scheme. Don't be afraid. *Never* be afraid to approach God.

He is a good, good Father, and we are His dearly beloved children. He only wants the best for each and every one of us. He promises.

Lord, we are flawed, yet Your mercy endures forever. Forgive us, guide us, shepherd us, and show us the way. Show us Your way. Amen.

Hold on Loosely

A generous person will prosper; whoever refreshes
others will be refreshed.

—Proverbs 11:25(New International Version)

DO YOU REMEMBER playing in sand as a child, maybe in
your backyard or at the beach or shore?

If I close my eyes and sit for a spell, I can easily be transported
back there—the feel of the welcome June sun warming my little
shoulders and the back of my neck; the pebbles in the sand, poking
my bony kneecaps as I reach for a toy shovel; my brother nearby,
making puttering engine sounds with his lips as he builds "roads"
with his toy excavator.

Do you remember how the sand felt between your fingers?

Wet sand feels different than dry sand. You can squeeze a
handful of wet sand, and the grains clump together. If you keep
adding sand and water, you might build a fort or a castle for
passersby to admire, but an incoming wave or a rain shower may
destroy your creation.

Dry sand is airy. A handful is here, and then it's gone, blown
away by a sudden breeze or simply escaping through the spaces

between fingers. Few can deny the pleasing sensation of sand flowing through fingers, enticing us to repeatedly scoop up handful after handful, just to feel the tickle, sample the grit, savor the flow. Again and again. It is restful. Meditative, even.

Sometimes, I imagine God's blessings to be like grains of sand. There are times when we want to close our hands around them, hold onto them tightly, and keep them to ourselves. Enjoyable momentarily, perhaps, but not nearly as rewarding as when we open our hands and let the blessings flow directly from God through us and on to someone else.

We are blessed, you and I, so that we may bless others.

Let's try holding loosely to our blessings. When they land in our hands, let's release them instead of keeping them all for ourselves. Just as a pebble tossed into still water creates ripples that extend far across the lake, our shared blessings will create the same effect. Jesus told His disciples, "Whoever believes in Me will do the works I have been doing, and they will do even greater things than these" (John 14:12 NIV). Accomplishing "greater things" begins with holding loosely to our blessings. We may never know, on this side of heaven, just how many souls have benefited from our shared blessings. But just the act of sharing is a blessing itself. It feels good. Some might even call it divine.

Lord, thank You all Your many blessings. When my hands want to grasp, I know You will give me a nudge. And I thank You with my whole heart. Amen.

It's a Good Thing I'm Not God

"Martha, Martha," the Lord answered, "you are worried and upset about many things, but few things are needed—or indeed only one. Mary has chosen what is better, and it will not be taken away from her."

—Luke 10:41–42 (New International Version)

EVERY TIME THE Mary and Martha story comes up, I get antsy. Same with the parable of the Prodigal Son.

Dutiful Martha and the stay-at-home, dependable son would have made a good match. Both were responsible adults, making sure the work got done and done the right way. Both were hard workers, trying to earn a place of favor and staying on task.

In the meantime, Mr. too-big-for-his-britches Prodigal Son takes his inheritance early, blows it all on riotous living, and then comes groveling back to his father.

Miss Mary, caught up in the exciting prospect of having honored guests, abandons all the napkin-folding and table-setting duties to sit at the feet of Jesus, hanging on His every word.

You can probably guess what I am thinking. Couldn't Mary have done some prep work beforehand to relieve Martha a little?

Shouldn't the stay-at-home brother have been given a larger inheritance for his faithful service all those years?

No fair, I say. No fair at all!

I know I am totally missing the point of each of the lessons. Rather that celebrating his return, my humanness wants Dad to give Prodigal Son a good tongue-lashing and never let him live it down. And to pay for shirking her meal-prep duties, I'd have Mary sentenced to cleaning the dishes alone for the rest of the year.

Yes, we are all lucky that I am not God.

Isaiah 55:9 (KJV) reads, "For as the heavens are higher than the earth, so My ways are higher than your ways and My thoughts than your thoughts."

Unlike people who take offense and hold grudges, God forgives those of us who seek Him, regardless of the length and depth of our sin. He speaks truth into our lives, feeding us the spiritual food of His Word.

Whether we realize it or not, we thirst for this God. It is a thirst that can only be quenched when we drink of Him, the Living Water.

Intellectually, I understand the messages behind the Martha/Mary story and the parable of the Prodigal Son. I know what they mean, but I struggle. You see, God is still operating on my heart to remove those "not fair" barbs. I am so thankful that He is a gentle surgeon.

Lord, I need heart surgery more often than I think. Cleanse me, rinsing away anything that dulls the light of Your love shining out to others. Make my thoughts higher today and every day. Amen.

Fear of Needles

Be devoted to one another in love. Honor one
another above yourselves.

—Romans 12:10 (New International Version)

IT WAS NEARLY 7:30 a.m., and I was headed for my annual blood draw, hungry, thirsty, and on edge.

I'm ashamed to admit it, but I saw another car heading in the same direction, so I sped ahead, parked quickly, and got to the door before the other driver had turned off his ignition.

My excuse was that I wanted it over and done with.

Forgive me, Lord.

The wait was short, only about five minutes. My name was called, and I looked up to see a young woman waiting for me in the doorway—pastel scrubs, dark hair, all business. She directed me back to number four, and I seated myself in the chair and pulled my arm out of my cardigan. In the space of a few seconds, my brain was bombarded by totally irrational thoughts.

Are there germs on this chair? Are flu bugs floating in the atmosphere? Will she use a fresh needle? Does she have a thing against tall women over sixty? Do I need a mint? What if she's new and not really good with the needle? What if I pass out?

These thoughts were interrupted when the phlebotomist stepped into the cubicle. She quickly verified my information on the computer screen to my left as I tried to evaluate her from her profile. I hoped to make eye contact, but it was impossible from the angle. All I saw was the side of her lovely, young face; her name tag that read "My name is April"; and her beautifully manicured left hand.

As she turned to me and tied the band around my upper arm, she began to sing under her breath. I didn't recognize the song, but I did recognize that it was a praise-and-worship tune, and her voice, though soft and low, was as sweet as a nightingale's.

"I'll try to give you a good vein," I said, eyeing my arm helplessly.

"You just relax," she replied.

Reassured by her presence and her voice, I exhaled, and it was over in a heartbeat.

"You are good!" I said, as she handed me the little cup and directed me toward my next task.

"Thank you," she said with a brilliant smile.

As I was leaving, I saw April, busy with another patient, but I stage-whispered to her, "Thank you for blessing me with your singing."

April's smile lit up her cubicle and bounced off the ceiling.

Thank you, Lord, for blessing me with April.

I didn't deserve April. Remember, I was the selfish one who rushed the door to get ahead of the other patient.

The world would say, "You should be punished for that behavior. You should have gotten the meanest, least-skilled phlebotomist in the place to stab your arm and leave a big bruise to remind you how selfish you were to rush ahead of that man."

But our God knows us through and through. He's not surprised by anything we do. He loves us unconditionally and is ever quick to forgive when we ask.

When I was nervous, He gave me April's song to remind me of who I am and who He is.

Psalm 56:3 (English Revised Version) reads, "When I am afraid, I put my trust in You." If we take that verse and replace the word "afraid" with any of our sins or needs, the result will be the same:

When I am *selfish*, I put my trust in You. When I am *greedy*, I put my trust in You. When I am *weak*, I put my trust in You. When I am *angry*, I put my trust in You. When I am *lonely*, I put my trust in You.

In his book *Ruthless Trust: The Ragamuffin's Path to God*, the late Brennan Manning writes:

> The splendor of a human heart that trusts it is loved unconditionally gives God more pleasure than Westminster Cathedral, the Sistine Chapel, Beethoven's 'Ninth Symphony', Van Gogh's 'Sunflowers", the sight of 10,000 butterflies in flight, or the scent of a million orchids in bloom. Trust is our gift back to God, and He finds it so enchanting that Jesus died for the love of it.

Trust is our gift to God. Imagine that.

Lord, we overthink, we complicate, and we struggle to please, constantly assess, evaluate, and compare. Release us, oh God, from our human tendencies, and teach us to trust You ruthlessly and with wild abandon. Amen.

Mistaken for a Mother

And Mary said, 'My soul magnifies the Lord, and my spirit rejoices in God my Savior, for He has looked on the humble estate of His servant. For behold, from now on all generations will call me blessed.'

—Luke 1:46–48 (English Standard Version)

THE SUN GLINTED on oily black feathers as the crow landed in the cabbage palm tree. I returned to my reading, but a couple of minutes later, the bird's movements once again caught my attention.

The crow was fumbling about in the interwoven basket-like bark on the side of the tree nearest me. When he raised his head, ready to take flight, I realized what he (or she) had been doing. In its beak was a light-colored, speckled orb—a mockingbird's egg.

As the crow took flight, heading south, I yelled, "Scram!"

Too little, too late. The crow and the egg were gone.

I felt a muscular contraction, either real or emotional, right in the center of my gut, as I pictured the mama mockingbird returning to the nest to see an empty spot where her egg had been.

Were there other eggs in the nest?

Would she mourn this one lost egg?

The egg incident brought to mind Mother's Day. When you are a woman and you are not a mother, Mother's Day Sunday can be awkward.

I confess that in the past, I have feigned motherhood. I have smiled and accepted a flower or handmade card from little boys and girls as they moved about the church.

Otherwise, this could have been the scene:

The small boy of about six rushes over to me excitedly and presents me with a red carnation.

I look into those sweet, innocent eyes.

Me: "No, sweetie. I don't get one."

Little boy: "Here! For Mother's Day."

He extends his arm, full length, as pleased as if he'd grown it himself.

Me: "No, honey. I don't get one. I'm not a mother."

He smiles at me with an expression that says he thinks I am pulling his leg.

Little boy: "Uh-huh. Oh yes, you are." He nods his head. "Yes, yes, yes."

Me: "No, really. I'm not a mom."

He's still nodding in the affirmative but may be starting to get impatient. I can't be sure.

I am aware our little exchange has drawn attention. I can hear people in nearby pews murmuring. Folks are wondering, *What's up with that woman?*

The little guy is beginning to wear me down, and I think he picks up on it. Silent, he furrows his brow and cocks his little head sideways, like a confused toy poodle.

Me: "Really, I am no one's mom."

He looks me up and down, curious.

Little boy: "Why not?"

Me: "It's a long story, but trust me, sweetie. I am not a mom."

Puzzled, he hesitates, oblivious to the fact that we are holding up the service and all those Mother's Day lunch reservations.

He shifts from right foot to left and twirls the increasingly limp stem of the carnation between his stubby little fingers, stained now with green.

He's not ready to give up so easily.

I can almost hear the wheels turning in his head as his expression shifts. He's had a eureka moment. He smiles.

Little boy: "W-e-l-l ... are you a grandma?"

I've been outsmarted.

I laugh.

He laughs.

Me: "*Yes*, that's it. I'm a *grandma!*"

I don't know which of us is more relieved.

I reach for the carnation, and we share one last smile. Delighted, he skips up the center aisle as the organist begins to play the final number.

Holy God, may You lead, guide, and strengthen mothers and fathers, as well as people who fill the role of parent. Show them the way to be positive role models for their children and for all children in their lives. Let Your great love flow through them and through all generations. Amen.

The Gift Rejected

For God so loved the world that He gave His only begotten Son that whoever believes in Him should not perish but have eternal life.

—John 3:16 (New King James Version)

DRIVING THROUGH THE neighborhood on trash-pickup day, I see I am not alone in doing a pre-Christmas clean out. Rubbish bins overflow with broken and worn-out items, waiting for the big trash truck to haul it all away.

Last week, I dug through decorations and my closet. Broken and unusable items went in the trash or recycling. Then I gathered up extra Christmas lights and trimmings, unworn clothing, and unused kitchen gadgets and packed it all in bags and boxes and into my car. I even dragged out extra pieces of luggage, wiped off the dust, and checked for anything interesting left in the zippered pockets before I added them to my donate pile.

Come Saturday morning, I was up early and eager to head out to dispose of my giveaways. I was so pleased with myself, my sense of accomplishment, and my attitude of goodwill. I felt generous and productive. Liberated, even. The spirit of giving warmed my heart—or was that my ego?

The thrift store hadn't been open long when I pulled into the parking lot and popped the trunk. I loaded my arms with as many bags as I could carry and staggered to the door. That's where I stopped dead in my tracks.

A handwritten sign on the door read, "No donations until January."

What?

I read it again.

"No donations until January."

As I stood staring, my feathers fell.

But, but, but ...

The policy makes perfect sense. The store is small with no storage space. As donations enter the door, they are immediately priced and put out for sale.

But what about me? After all, it is all about me, right? I wanted—I *needed*—to unload this stuff *today*, not carry it around with me for another month. I thought I was benevolently sharing the overflow of my blessings as a gift to the thrift store and its customers, but my plan was foiled. Deflated, I loaded it all into my car and drove away.

God is so gracious. He saw my ego operating here but did not hold it against me.

Driving home, I began to think about times in my life when I have witnessed gifts not graciously received or even rejected. I've done it myself.

The Christmas I was in eighth grade, among my presents were two sweaters my mom had spent hours shopping for (in a blizzard in heels, she said) and was unable to conceal my horror at her selection of colors and styles. One was a pretty azure color, but it was a bulky-knit turtleneck with a knitted belt that made even my bean-pole figure look like a shapeless roll of bologna with a head. The other, also a turtleneck, wasn't so bulky, but the color was an unflattering shade of mustard gold. From then on, I was allowed to pick out my own clothing gifts. As an apology to my mother for my rude behavior, I voluntarily, albeit grudging, wore the ugly sweaters anyway.

For whatever reason, some people have a hard time accepting gifts. Take them flowers, and they say they have allergies. Give them something you think they'd like, and they examine it closely and then hand it back to you, saying, "I would never use/wear/eat this. You take it."

And then there's the but-I-didn't-get-you-anything scenario. When surprised by a gift, we may feel bad for not having a gift for the giver. Is it any wonder that we think we must earn or buy our salvation?

Jesus is the exception to the rule, He who gave His life so we might live. Jesus is the free gift, so precious that it could never be earned, even if we labored for a thousand years. When He walked the earth for thirty-three years, he was 100 percent God and 100 percent man, yet without sin. Any temptation you have confronted, Jesus, in His earthly personage, experienced as well. Not in the same scenario, perhaps, but Jesus experienced suffering equal to or greater than anything we could ever go through in our lives.

Jesus knows what it feels like to be rejected. To have His gift rejected.

Jesus offers the greatest gift humankind has ever known.

You can't put a price tag on it. You can't put it in a box and wrap it with paper.

You can accept the gift for yourself. You can't accept it on behalf of another, but you can share with another person the good news about the gift. You can't hold it in your hands, but you can hold it in your heart. Now and forever.

Lord God, Father of all creation, thank You for Jesus. We are not worthy, but we accept and believe and praise Your holy name. Amen.

What Did Jesus Really Look Like?

And the Word became flesh and dwelt among us, and we have seen His glory, glory as of the only Son from the Father, full of grace and truth.

—John 1:14 (English Standard Version)

THE HIGHLY PUBLICIZED trial was in week number two. The next witness up was a congressman who I had seen for years in campaign and news photos but never in person. He approached from the back of the courtroom, conservatively dressed in a tailored dark suit and crisp white shirt. He arrived in front of my desk, and, without looking up, I asked that he state his name for the court's record. When I finished writing out his name, I said, "Would you please raise your right hand to be sworn?"

It was my practice to always look the witness in the eye when I administered the oath. When I looked up and made eye contact with the congressman, I lost all conscious train of thought.

His striking appearance up close took me by surprise. When I was supposed to be swearing him to tell the truth, the whole truth, and nothing but the truth, I was thinking, *Wow. I always thought he had brown eyes. They're blue. Light, sparkly, interestingly blue. They look really nice with his dark hair. And that hint of silver in his hair makes his eyes even more striking. Wow, I had no idea he was this handsome.*

I refocused about the time I said, "Please take a seat on the witness stand."

Now, my colleagues assured me later that I gave the oath without a hitch, but you could not prove it by me. Between the words "to be sworn" and "take a seat on the witness stand," I was distracted by the unexpected beauty of this man's face.

Embarrassing but not surprising, according to experts.

Humans are naturally drawn to beauty. It happens every day. One can't help noticing and admiring physically attractive people. It is scientific fact. Even infants younger than six months of age are drawn to the more attractive of two facial photographs 80 percent of the time, according to a 2004 study at the University of Exeter, as reported by the British Broadcasting Corporation.

Why else do we, both women and men, spend so much time and money on clothing, cosmetics, salon treatments, and plastic surgery? We all want to be attractive—aesthetically pleasing to ourselves and to others.

That is why I found verse two of the fifty-third chapter of Isaiah utterly astounding.

The New King James version reads: "For He shall grow up before Him as a tender plant and as a root out of dry ground. He has no form or comeliness; And when we see Him, there *is* no beauty that we should desire Him."

Shocking, isn't it?

Regardless of how Christ has been depicted by artists and movie makers throughout history, according to this scripture, our Savior was not physically attractive. Christ was not a "pretty face" commanding attention with his brilliant smile. He was not some handsome celebrity, wowing people with his rugged good looks, boyish charm, and sharply tailored robes.

Yet people were—and still are—drawn to Him.

People were drawn and *we* are drawn to Him because of who He is and not how He looked.

Just as He came to earth as a helpless infant, He walked the land, clothed in the skin and wearing the face of a regular guy. Dusty sandals, wrinkled robe, sweaty brow. Based on looks alone, He'd never get a second glance. The world's greatest gift wrapped in rough linen.

His divinity is what draws us to Him. God became man, supreme sacrifice, Great Physician, best friend, provider, constant companion, the same yesterday, today, and forever. Light of the world, casting out darkness throughout the universe and, especially, from our very own hearts.

Powerful, my friends. Powerful beyond words.

Although I still admire and appreciate the artists' renderings of Christ as golden, haloed, and handsome, I have to say that, today, I love Him even more, knowing that He would never be voted one of *People* magazine's World's Most Beautiful People. On the outside, He looked like a regular guy. But on the inside, He was pure God, "full of grace and truth." What a perfect example of the saying, "It's not what's on the outside that matters but what's on the inside."

Lord, thank You for Your Word that never fails to enlighten. Draw me close, Lord. Create a hunger in me to study Your Word, that I may glorify You forever. Amen.

A Bright Spot in a Pandemic

Children are a heritage from the Lord, offspring a
reward from Him.

—Psalm 127:3–5 (New International Version)

A FRIENDLY YOUNG couple bought a house up the street
from us a couple of years back. We met them when they strolled
past our house, walking their dogs. We normally saw them, Jeff
and Ellen, walking on weekends, midmorning, and they often
paused a moment for a chat.

When the pandemic arrived, we continued to visit with them
but this time from across the street, in order to practice safe
distancing. In the spring, it became apparent that Ellen's gait had
changed. She was moving a little slower, and so was Jeff. Could it
be? It would be rude to ask, of course, but we wondered, *Is Ellen
now eating for two?* Before long, Jeff could no longer keep the news
to himself. They were, indeed, expecting, and it wouldn't be long.

As the due date in early June drew near, Jeff and Ellen
continued their evening strolls but at an even slower pace. Jeff's
blue eyes twinkled with anticipation of the arrival of their first
child, a daughter they would call Savannah.

Mid-June, we saw Jeff at their mailbox. He was beside himself. The baby had arrived, safe and healthy, and Ellen was doing great. Jeff was so thrilled that he was practically levitating.

My husband got to see the baby first, since he spends more time outside than I do. They pushed the stroller by on an evening walk, and he got a glimpse of the most beautiful blue eyes he had ever seen.

Fast-forward a week. I was taking the recycling out to the curb when I saw them halfway past our house. I called out, "It's the baby!" I strode toward them and stopped short, remembering to keep my social distance.

There she was, lying in the stroller, six months old, big blue eyes with a wisp of sandy hair peeking out of her tiny hooded jacket. She looked at me with great curiosity; then she looked at her mother questioningly, as if to say, "Do I know this person?"

Daddy Jeff said, "Yes, sweetie, there are other people in the world." We adults laughed.

Of all the hardships the world endured during the pandemic, this little family received a miracle of epic proportions. Not only did they experience the beauty of having their first child, but global circumstances required they stay home, in the house, with this baby every day of her little life. No choosing between working or parenting. No finding the appropriate day care. No tearful goodbyes at leaving this most precious gift in the hands of strangers. Mom and Dad being able to be with this child every day is such a precious gift that it brings tears to my eyes just thinking about it.

I hope this story makes you smile. I hope it lifts your heart as you picture this sweet little family, all nestled safely in their home.

Jeff and Ellen's story is not an isolated incident. Other stories are out there. You likely won't find them in the newspaper or on TV. But I know for certain that in the midst of calamity, if we look for it, we will see the magnitude of God's presence and great love for us.

As I recall looking into little Savannah's eyes that day, I feel an overwhelming sense of hope. It rises up in me like the morning mist on a mountain lake. My heart is full and my spirit calm. And, just like Jeff and Ellen, I am extraordinarily blessed.

Holy God, Christ is the author and finisher of our faith. Remind us to look for everyday miracles, and help us spread hope to all we encounter. Amen.

Look into His Eyes

The lamp of the body is the eye.

—Matthew 6:22 (New King James Version)

FROM MY SEAT in the back, I watched the young woman move about the front of the meeting room. She seemed to be very popular as she greeted people with a handshake, a hug or a wave, and a smile. I guessed her age as late twenties or early thirties. Her look was understated. Very little makeup. Stylish print tunic over navy slacks. On her feet, she wore beige pointed-toed pumps with heels just high enough that she stood eye to eye with most people in the room. No jewelry, except for tasteful little earrings. Her chin-length hair was swept back in a no-nonsense ponytail that emphasized her flawless skin and big round eyes. Her eyes were remarkable. The kind of eyes that draw you in.

As she continued to work her way toward the back of the room, I whispered to my husband, "Now, *that* is a politician."

She also was an elected official, so her persona served her well.

That got me to thinking about Jesus and how He worked crowds. Or, actually, how He didn't.

During His earthly ministry, as He traveled the region we call the Holy Land, Jesus was not campaigning. This was no public relations event. Word had spread. People knew who He was.

Jesus was pursued by thousands. People sought Him out to hear His message, to be healed of their many afflictions, and, ultimately, to be set free from oppression and sin.

Others would pursue Him in order to silence Him and did so in the most public and humiliating way possible.

This morning, I imagined Jesus on the road, not as children's Bible stories illustrate but as a dusty and sweaty traveler. His robes were sweat-stained, and His feet were calloused and dusty. His face was weathered from hours of walking in the sun, and His hair and beard grew wild and untamed. Oh, but His eyes …

They must have been remarkable, don't you think?

His eyes revealed a light that was within Him, a light that surrounded Him and that emanated from His entire being. Ancient alien theorists would call this evidence of an extraterrestrial. We Christ followers call it God robed in flesh, come to save us all.

Lord Jesus, thank You for reminding me of the reality of Your earthly life and of the power of Your presence in my life. Amen.

The Lady from Buffalo

Humble yourselves before the Lord, and He will lift you up.

—James 4:10 (New International Version)

ON A MIDMORNING stroll along the sand, Mom and I came upon a woman sitting in a beach chair, facing the horizon. From early morning until past sunset, the beach was dotted with tourists in their chairs, especially in midwinter, the height of tourist season. But this lady was not on the sand. She sat waist-deep in the fifty-degree Gulf of Mexico, gazing at the horizon. And she was smiling.

Seeing her made me smile.

"You must be from up North," I called to her.

Her smile broadened. "It was minus-thirty when I left home." Home was Buffalo, New York.

We all laughed. I gave her a thumbs-up and a big grin as we walked on by.

Mom loves to walk on the beach. We'd waited for over a month for the perfect day to take our first beach walk.

"How long has it been since you walked on the beach?" Mom asked.

I was slow to answer. Slightly embarrassed, I tried to remember. "Mmm, eight months, maybe."

You may wonder how I can possibly live within a mile of the cerulean waters of the Gulf of Mexico and not walk its white-sand beaches daily. The answer is simple; I am spoiled. For the past eight years, I have lived here, a place where the sun shines nearly every day and where flowers bloom year-round. Folks dream all year about coming here for one short week of vacation, but I wake up here every day.

Floridians know they are lucky, but may not appreciate the climate quite as much as those of us who have spent years up North—or the tourists who come here to get warm, like the smiling lady in the beach chair.

You see, when every day is sunshine, you might just take it for granted.

Our faith walk is similar. What would the journey be without the highs and the lows? You might think, *I wouldn't mind everything being good all the time.* But we learn the true value of faith in God when we are confronted with the bad stuff that life sometimes delivers.

Years ago, when difficulties arose in my life, I would pray, "Lord, please get me out of this!" I wanted out. Like a little child. *Daddy, please make it go away!* But then one day, out of the blue, my prayer was different: "Lord, show me Your wisdom in this situation." In other words, *God, I know You've got this. Show me what You want me to learn.*

I'm convinced these words did not originate with me. I still had that get-me-out-of-this mindset. But God was changing my heart. I was growing spiritually and learning to trust Him.

Every challenge, every physical, emotional, or spiritual ice storm, blizzard, or hurricane is an opportunity for us to humble ourselves before God and say, "Here I am, Lord. I surrender this battle to You. Speak to my heart and guide me in thought, word, and deed. I love You, and I trust You."

Once the dust settles, God's wisdom will be revealed to you, like sunbeams breaking through dark clouds, and you will know that it was God who brought you through.

Life's not easy, and stuff happens. But God is faithful. Know that He doesn't want to just lend you a hand. He wants to carry you in His mighty and loving arms.

Lord, You are with me in the good times, and I often forget to thank You for that. When hard times come, remind me to humble myself and surrender to Your will in all things, big and small, so I may learn from You and grow. Amen.

I Feel Bad about My Feet

I will offer You my grateful heart, for I am Your
unique creation, filled with wonder and awe. You
have approached even the smallest details with
excellence; Your works are wonderful; I carry this
knowledge deep within my soul.

—Psalm 139:14 (The Voice)

I FEEL BAD about my feet. Wait—let me correct that. I used to feel bad about my feet. For about thirty-five years, I felt ashamed, embarrassed, and sad.

Why? Because by society's standards, my feet were too big. No, I mean it. The largest size most shoe companies make are size 10. In recent years, they've added size 11. Still too small. I wear a size 12, and I won't be offended if, the next time you see me, your eyes stray downward. It's OK. Really.

Never mind that my feet are well in proportion with my height (which I have always refused to feel bad about); you won't see me wearing ankle bracelets or toe rings. As a matter of fact, I only started wearing capri pants in the past eight years because I feared they would draw attention to my gargantuan podiatric marvels.

In 2006, filmmaker Nora Ephron wrote a book called *I Feel Bad about My Neck: And Other Thoughts on Being a Woman.* When I read it, I realized I was not alone because, in addition to my feet, I felt bad about my neck too.

About that same time, Candice Bergen began wearing scarves to awards show.

"Aha! Look at that. Candice Bergen feels bad about her neck too!" I declared to no one in particular.

Do you have a body part you feel bad about? Most of us do. It's OK to admit it.

Why do you feel bad?

For a variety of reasons. You were criticized by someone during your lifetime whose opinion mattered to you—a family member, a friend, the most popular but most self-centered person in school.

Or you compare yourself to airbrushed images in magazines. (I was relieved when I saw a cosmetic ad recently of the lovely British actress Helen Mirren, age seventy-four, where I could actually see some pores in her skin.) Or you compare yourself to your genetically blessed neighbor, who looks as young as her daughter. Or any person or institution that makes you feel any less than the perfect creation you actually are.

I had a revelation about my feet one Sunday during worship service. It was one of those out-of-the-blue occurrences, as if God reached down and tweaked my right ear.

If I could have heard actual words rather than the message to my heart, here's what God would have said:

"Your feet were specially designed to give you the stability that you need in life. These feet I gave you will take you to all the places I want you to go. These feet, your feet, will let you dance for joy and will serve you well all the days of your life. A smaller pair just would not do."

I was embarrassed by my shallowness.

So I no longer feel bad about my feet. I love them. Should someone comment on their size, I'll not be become arrogant and puffed up; I promise.

And for any of us who feel bad about our necks or any other body part, let's just tape these words to our bathroom mirrors:

Lord, I offer You my grateful heart, for I am Your unique creation, full of beauty, strength, and love. Amen.

Don't Be Fooled by Golf Balls

Who teaches us more than the beasts of the earth,
and makes us wiser than the birds of the heavens?

—Job 35:11 (New King James Version)

THE TREE TRIMMER scaled the ladder with speed and agility. With a harness wrapped around his hips, he deftly wielded the chainsaw, first in his right hand and then his left, performing a kind of aerial dance as he trimmed away the lower palm fronds, dropping them with precision to fall inside the fence, rather than into the bay.

A couple of years ago, Mom and I watched with fascination as this same fellow scaled and trimmed a gargantuan Cuban laurel tree next door. Our seven palm trees were child's play for him, compared to that behemoth.

In the midst of his trimming, he tossed a bright yellow golf ball into the pebbles below. Then, another one. Two yellow golf balls in a palm tree?

The culprits?

Crows.

I may have told you about watching a battle between a

mockingbird and a crow, as the mockingbird fought to protect her nest and its contents.

Crows, apparently, think golf balls look a lot like bird eggs. The yellow balls are used at a miniature golf course half a mile away. The day after the tree trim, I saw a crow flying into one of the palms with a white golf ball in its beak, stowing it for noshing later.

What a lesson those crows can teach! I could not help but think about all the times in my life that I have been misled by golf balls or fool's gold.

Whether spoken aloud or not, there have been times when I've thought life would be perfect if _____ (fill in the blank). But when the goal is finally achieved or the object of my yearning is finally in my possession, I realize that the happiness or security or esteem I expected it to bring is like that yellow golf ball masquerading as an egg. Pretty but without substance or sustenance.

Our most precious commodity is time. How much time have I wasted, longing for, pursuing, and then being disappointed by yellow golf balls?

I love the Apostle Paul's advice to the church at Philippi. The New Living Translation of Philippians 4:8 reads, "Fix your thoughts on what is true, and honorable, and right, and pure, and lovely, and admirable. Think about things that are excellent and worthy of praise."

I'm not surprised that yellow golf balls or their equivalents do not make the list. Are you?

Lord God, You rein us in when we need it, and for that, I am so thankful. May the scales fall away from our eyes that we may see Your wisdom and glory in the smallest of things. Amen.

Accept Your God-given Beauty

You are altogether beautiful, my darling; there is
no flaw in you.

—Song of Songs 4:7 (New International Version)

GOD LOVES YOU without makeup. When you roll out of bed
with morning breath; puffy, squinty eyes; and a terrible case of
bed-head, God thinks you are perfect. And you are.

You are perfection, "fearfully and wonderfully made," created
by the Master Artist. But we don't see as God sees. We judge our
beauty or physical appearance by the standards of our culture and
always, always, *always* find ourselves wanting.

I remember the first time I ever saw a supermodel sans makeup.
Whoa! Scary, right? But actually, she looked just like us when we
get up in the morning, or on a day off, or after a hospitalization.
Our private face, our vulnerable face. Not a Facebook face.

What is beauty? Our culture tells us that the enhanced,
airbrushed version with heavy makeup, faux lashes, implants, and
hair extensions is true beauty. When leafing through magazines,
we envy their hair, their flawless skin, their curves or lack thereof,
when, in reality, it is mostly illusion.

Don't get me wrong. My vanity keeps me coloring my gray hair, putting on some makeup, and trying to be well groomed. In recent years, however, I've backed away from women's magazines. No longer do I buy into the idea that a woman with a face bare of makeup is ugly.

Last Sunday's sermon touched on our culture's unrealistic expectations. Adequate is passé. Enough is never enough. Everything has to be huge, gigantic, colossal. If it's not new and improved, forget about it. We want everything and everyone to be awesome, including ourselves.

Rarely can we look at an untouched photograph and appreciate the God-given beauty, whether looking at a face or of a landscape. Our eyes want a quick fix so we can move on. When we pause, linger on the image, study the intricacy of design, appreciate the individuality, see its history and its future, and view it from God's loving perspective, we will be changed by what we see.

Even when we look in the mirror.

Years ago, I had a one-line prayer taped to the mirror in my bedroom. It read, "Dear God, help me to see others as You created them." Today, let's pray this one together:

Dear God, let me see other people, including myself, as You see us. Amen.

The Bible Study

When You said, "Seek My face," My heart said to
You, "Your face, Lord, I will seek."

—Psalm 27:8 (New King James Version)

A NEW BIBLE study is beginning. Holding the study book in
my hand, I admire the soft pinks and purples and the delicate
fonts on the cover. On three separate occasions, I had opened
it and had begun to read but was interrupted each time by life
circumstances. With great determination, I take the book, my
Bible, and a pen and settle in for some serious study. Serious,
meaning committed. Whatever that looks like today.

The word *study* can stir memories of working to meet
deadlines and demands—challenging school projects, prepping
for qualifying examinations, or filing a report your boss dropped
on your desk at the last minute. Given enough coffee and sugar,
I've always worked well under deadlines, but I know some people
actually freeze in their tracks.

The first challenge when you encounter any instructor or boss
for the very first time is, "What exactly does he or she want?"

Once you've figured that out, you are golden. There's nothing more disheartening than hearing, "No. That's not right. That's not what I wanted."

Ugh!

But here's the good news: God is pleased with whatever manner you choose or with whatever manner you are able to study the Word. Just the fact that you desire to know Him better will motivate you to seek Him. Like me, you may find that the amount of time and energy invested in Bible study is directly related to how much you grow in your spiritual walk and how much more you want to learn.

The precious facilitator of this new Bible study is tuned into God's heart. She's made it very user-friendly. No huge demands, just a schedule of pages to be discussed each week. Even the basic suggested requirement for participation is simply showing up, praying for each other, and listening. How beautiful is that? No homework, unless you want it.

With that predicate, I pick up the book every couple of days at different times during the day. Some of the verses seem new to me—all about how beloved we are. The book's "reflection questions" really challenge me. As expected, my muscles tense as my mind automatically goes to, "What is the correct answer to this?"

Wait a minute. I have to reset my thinking. There are no right or wrong answers here. The simple but powerful act of reading and reflecting are steps forward spiritually, chances to grow in my understanding of God and in my relationship with Him. It's all part of the journey.

So I am setting aside my preconceived notions about studies and incorrect answers and pop quizzes. I am diving into this Bible study. Some weeks, I may be totally submerged, while other weeks, I may only dip my toe in, but you know what? It is all good. And to God be the glory!

Lord, we make things so complicated. Help us to seek You, oh God, one verse at a time, with simplicity, open minds, and joy. Amen.

Some Final Thoughts

I WATCH FROM the window as our fifteen-year-old Jack Russell terrier rolls and writhes like a puppy in the freshly spread mulch. She wiggles and squirms, and, after several minutes, she flips upright, punctuating her rollicking routine with a resounding, full-body sneeze. I know how she feels. Knowing that God really, really likes me makes me want to do something similar. Just last week, my mom and I, still in our pajamas, danced all around the kitchen. Our only accompaniment was our off-key singing and the music in our hearts. We'd felt like dancing, so we did.

Knowing that God really, really likes you makes you want to dance. And sing. And hop and skip and jump, like the baby goats in those YouTube videos we love to watch. Your spirit will soar like a bird on the wing. It's such a marvelous feeling!

People who know that God really, really likes them understand the difference between fleeting happiness and deep-seated joy. When you know that God really, really likes you, you have true, unfettered hope—hope that instills in you a confidence far beyond anything you could ever achieve on your own. If you find that hard to believe, just read John 14:12. Seriously, I would not make this up.

After the night when I came to Christ, kneeling by my bed, I felt as light as a feather, freed from burdens I never knew I carried. I was overcome with peace, love, and a sense of hope for the future.

In the days that followed, I became confused. I realized that other than the prayer of confession I had made, I had no idea how to pray. I am a rules-and-regulations kind of gal. Questions flooded my mind. What was I supposed to say? How was I to address God? Should I address God formally, with the appropriate use of "Thee" and "Thou," or was plain old everyday language acceptable? Was I supposed to kneel? What should I do with my hands? Should my eyes be open or closed? Was it selfish to pray for myself? Did I need to do it out loud, should I whisper, or could I just think my prayers?

Desperate, I headed to the nearest bookstore and bought a small book by Pastor Charles Stanley called *Handle with Prayer*. It was just what I needed at the time, and I still have it.

If you want to pray but don't know how, an easy acronym to remember is ACTS. A stands for *adoration*, as in, "Our Father, who art in heaven, hallowed be thy name." C stands for *confession*, where we confess to God our sins. T stands for *thanksgiving*, when we thank God for our many blessings. S is for *supplication*, where we offer up prayer for others as well as ourselves.

I've heard people say, "I want to pray for [insert name or situation], but I don't know what to pray for." Never mind about that. Rest assured that God knows precisely what that person or situation needs. Don't be intimidated by which words to use. Just the sound of your voice gives God the greatest joy.

After all, He really, really likes you!

The Beckoning

DO YOU FEEL disconnected from the divine, unanchored, or discontented? Do you have a deep yearning within that you just can't seem to satisfy, despite your best efforts? Are you exhausted from carrying the burdens of modern-day living? Do you feel isolated, hopeless, and alone? Have you ever felt an internal stirring to break free from emotional and spiritual bondage?

If you have, you are not alone. I have been all of these and more. I believed in God, but I thought if I entered into a relationship with Him or "got religion," I would have to give up all the things I liked to do, and I wouldn't like the new me. Was I ever wrong! My only regret has been that I didn't make the decision sooner.

So how do you respond to the beckoning, that stirring within you? First and foremost, your desire must come from your heart and soul, not your head. You cannot rationalize the Holy Spirit's drawing you into a relationship with the divine God. When you've bottomed out, hit the wall, or simply grown bone-tired of fighting life's battles alone, you are ready to surrender to the One who wants you to have the life for which you were created. That's when, from your heart, you pray, "Dear God, I believe in You and I trust You. I believe in Jesus Christ, Your only Son, who died on the cross for my sins. Forgive me of my sins and make me new. I want to live for You from this day forward. Amen." You may pray all or some of these words over and over as you allow the Holy Spirit to cleanse you. Let go of your anger, resentment, shame and regret. Release everything that weighs you down. Every last thing.

What's next? You may feel different instantly or it may be gradual change. Either way, get ready for a radical change. You've undergone spiritual heart surgery, having shed no blood of your own. You are forgiven. You are set free. Your record is expunged. Your past is behind you.

The new you has the power to change the world. How?

Having entered into relationship with God through the sacrifice of Jesus, you become a living, breathing conduit for the boundlessly powerful love of God. On our own, It is humanly impossible, but through God we, you and I, can do the impossible. We can change the world, beginning with our very own families and extending it into our communities.

I am living proof that an insecure and unanchored life can be changed by God's mighty love. I pray that someday, maybe today, you hear the beckoning, accept the call and assume your identity as the person God created you to be. I promise you will never regret it. Angels will rejoice and so will I.

Questions to Ponder

It is my privilege to share these stories with you, and I invite you to consider these questions for reflection, on your own or with a friend:

1. Have your ideas about or understanding of God changed over the course of your lifetime? If so, how? If so, to what do you attribute the change(s)?

2. Have you ever struggled with grasping the divine love of God? Have you ever had to explain it to another, adult or child? Had you ever considered the idea of God liking as well as loving you? Do you believe there is a difference?

3. What does the Genesis 1:12 verse mean to you? How can we employ the words of the verse to relate more kindly to people who are different from ourselves?

4. Does knowing that God likes you change your image of God?

5. Did any of the stories resonate with you personally? If so, which one(s) and why?

Bibliography

Ephron, Nora. *I Feel Bad about My Neck.* New York: Vintage Books, 2008.

Manning, Brennan. *Ruthless Trust: The Ragamuffin's Path to God.* New York: HarperCollins, 2009.

Peterson, Eugene. *Eat This Book: A Conversation in the Art of Spiritual Reading.* Grand Rapids, MI: William B. Eerdmans Publishing Co., 2009.

Stanley, Charles. *Handle with Prayer: Unwrap the Source of God's Strength for Living.* Colorado Springs, CO: Victor Books, 1992.

Acknowledgments

This book would not have been possible without the encouragement and help from many precious individuals. I offer my gratitude to my parents for giving me life and my husband for making it both fun and interesting; to my high school English teacher, Mrs. Connie Davis, as pretty as she was kind, for her inspiring comments on my writing; to my two soul sisters, Trisha and Christine Marie, my precious sisters by other mothers; to Pasadena Community Church for paving the way for my classes; and last but certainly not least, my yoga ladies, Beth, Rose, Hazel, Judy and Judi, Jan, Cheri, Linda, Karen, Kim, Sandy, Lisa, Shari, Bobbie, Betty, Sally, Shirley, Janet, Cathy, Denise, Beverly, Nancy and Nancy, Eileen, Dawn, Marilyn, Helen, Donna, Evelyn, Pat, Joan, Patti, Sallie, Mary, Sherri, Susan and Susan, Ella, Marie, Jo, Janet, Julia, and Annie and my sister-in-law Patricia. You shower me with love and support, and I thank God for each one of you.

Printed in the United States
by Baker & Taylor Publisher Services